Drawing and Learning About Fashion

Using Shapes and Lines

written and illustrated by
Amy Bailey Muehlenhardt

Thanks to our advisers for their expertise, research, and advice:

Linda Frichtel, Design Adjunct Faculty, MCAD
Minneapolis, Minnesota

Susan Kesselring, M.A., Literacy Educator
Rosemount–Apple Valley–Eagan (Minnesota) School District

PICTURE WINDOW BOOKS
Minneapolis, Minnesota

D1208355

Amy Bailey Muehlenhardt
grew up in Fergus Falls, Minnesota,
and attended Minnesota State
University in Moorhead. She holds
a Bachelor of Science degree in
Graphic Design and Art Education.
Before coming to Picture Window
Books, Amy was an elementary art
teacher. She always impressed upon
her students that "everyone is an artist."
Amy lives in Mankato, Minnesota,
with her husband, Brad, and
daughter, Elise.

For Elise Lauren, my new smile.
ABM

Editorial Director: Carol Jones
Managing Editor: Catherine Neitge
Creative Director: Keith Griffin
Editor: Jill Kalz
Editorial Adviser: Bob Temple
Story Consultant: Terry Flaherty
Designer: Jaime Martens
Page Production: Picture Window Books
The illustrations in this book were created with pencil
and colored pencil.

Picture Window Books
5115 Excelsior Boulevard
Suite 232
Minneapolis, MN 55416
1-877-845-8392
www.picturewindowbooks.com

Printed in the United States of America.

Library of Congress Cataloging-in-Publication Data
Muehlenhardt, Amy Bailey, 1974–
Drawing and learning about fashion / written and illustrated by
Amy Bailey Muehlenhardt.
p. cm. — (Sketch it!)
Includes bibliographical references and index.
ISBN 1-4048-1191-5 (hardcover)
1. Fashion drawing—Juvenile literature. 2. Clothing and dress—
History—20th century—Juvenile literature. I. Title: Fashion.
II. Title.
TT509.M84 2005
741.6'72—dc22   2005007173

Table of Contents

Everyone Is an Artist

There is no right or wrong way to draw!

With a little patience and some practice, anyone can learn to draw. Did you know every picture begins as a simple shape? If you can draw shapes, you can draw anything.

The Basics of Drawing

line—a long mark made by a pen, a pencil, or another tool

guideline—a line used to help you draw; the guideline will be erased when your drawing is almost complete

shade—to color in with your pencil

value—the lightness or darkness of an object

shape—the form or outline of an object or figure

diagonal—a shape or line that leans to the side

4

Before you begin, you will need

a pencil,
an eraser,
lots of paper!

Four Tips for Drawing

1. Draw very lightly.

Try drawing light, medium, and dark lines. The softer you press, the lighter the lines will be.

2. Draw your shapes.

When you are finished drawing, connect your shapes with a sketch line.

3. Add details.

Details are small things that make a good picture even better.

4. Color your art.

Use your colored pencils, crayons, or markers to create backgrounds.

Let's get started!

Simple shapes help you draw.

Practice drawing these shapes before you begin.

 **circle**
A circle is round like a ball.

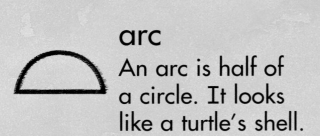 **oval**
An oval is a circle with its cheeks sucked in.

arc
An arc is half of a circle. It looks like a turtle's shell.

 **square**
A square has four equal sides and four corners.

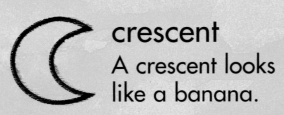 **crescent**
A crescent looks like a banana.

 **triangle**
A triangle has three sides and three corners.

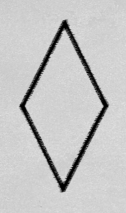 **diamond**
A diamond is two triangles put together.

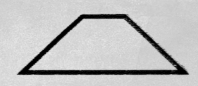 **trapezoid**
A trapezoid has four sides and four corners. Two of its sides are different lengths.

 **rectangle**
A rectangle has two long sides, two short sides, and four corners.

You will also use lines when drawing.

Practice drawing these lines.

vertical
A vertical line stands tall like a tree.

zigzag
A zigzag line is sharp and pointy.

horizontal
A horizontal line lies down and takes a nap.

wavy
A wavy line moves up and down like a roller coaster.

diagonal
A diagonal line leans to the side.

Remember to practice drawing.

While using this book, you may want to stop drawing at step five or six. That's great! Everyone is at a different drawing level.

dizzy
A dizzy line spins around and around.

Don't worry if your picture isn't perfect. The important thing is to have fun.

Be creative!

The Flapper Dress

Flappers were fashionable, free-spirited women who danced the night away at jazz clubs in the late 1920s. They wore short dresses without much shape and no sleeves. Flapper dresses were often decorated with beads, sequins, or feathers.

Step 1

Draw an oval for the head and a rectangle for the dress.

Step 2

Draw two vertical lines for the neck. Add an arc for the hat. Draw two diagonal lines for the neckline of the dress.

Step 3

Draw a horizontal line for the slip beneath the dress. Add two curved lines for the sash. Draw diagonal lines for the fringes.

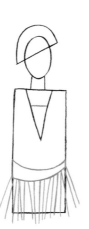

Step 4

Draw two diagonal lines for the hat ribbon. Add wavy lines for the hair.

Step 5

Define the hat and dress with a sketch line. Draw three rectangles for the arms. Draw two rectangles for the legs. Add two arcs for the hands.

Step 6

Erase the extra lines. Add details such as a face, a necklace, a feather boa, and shoes.

Step 7

Color your person and add a background.

Plus Fours

Plus fours were a popular style of pants for men in the 1930s, especially on the golf course. The pants were gathered just below the knee and puffed out. Men wore long, thin socks tucked up under their plus fours.

Step 1

Draw two ovals for the body.

Step 2

Draw four ovals for the arms.

Step 3

Draw two rectangles for the pants. Add an oval for the head.

Step 4

Draw two circles and two rectangles for the legs. Add two ovals for the shoes.

Step 5

Define the outfit with a sketch line. Draw two triangles for the hands. Add two triangles for the collar.

Step 6

Erase the extra lines. Draw an oval for the hat. Add details such as a golf club, a golf ball, and curved lines for the pleats in the plus fours.

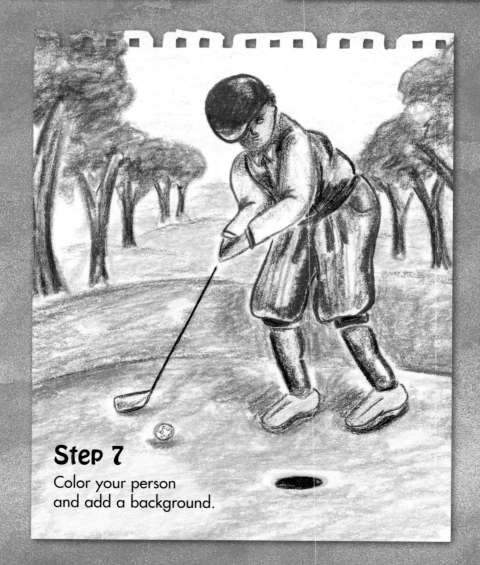

Step 7

Color your person and add a background.

The "Bar" Suit

In 1947, designer Christian Dior introduced a new look for women called the "Bar" suit. It included a full skirt and a fitted jacket with a tight waist. With World War II finally over, people wanted to celebrate life again by wearing fancy styles.

Step 1

Draw an arc for the shoulders and an oval for the head.

Step 2

Draw a triangle and a trapezoid for the body.

Step 3

Draw two vertical lines for the neck. Add a trapezoid for the skirt.

Step 4

Draw two triangles for the collar. Draw four ovals for the arms.

Step 5

Define the outfit with a sketch line. Draw two trapezoids for the hands. Add a vertical line down the middle of the jacket.

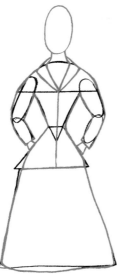

Step 6

Erase the extra lines. Add details such as a hat, a face, and boots. Draw diagonal and vertical lines for the pleats in the skirt.

Step 7

Color your person and add a background.

Black Leather Jacket

In the 1950s, many young men followed the look of such stars as James Dean and Elvis Presley. The "rebel" look included blue jeans, a tight white t-shirt, and a black leather jacket. Some men also wore penny loafers with this outfit and slicked back their hair.

Step 1

Draw a rectangle for the body. Add an oval for the head.

Step 2

Draw two vertical lines for the neck. Draw four ovals for the arms.

Step 3

Draw five rectangles for the jeans. Draw two ovals for the shoes.

Step 4

Draw two triangles for the collar. Add a curved line for the jacket zipper. Draw an oval for the hair.

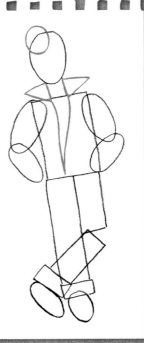

Step 5

Define the outfit with a sketch line. Draw two trapezoids for the hands. Add a curved line for the ear and the rest of the hair.

Step 6

Erase the extra lines. Add details such as a face, pockets, and a zipper on the jeans.

Step 7

Color your person and add a background.

Miniskirt

In the 1960s, many young women decided that they didn't want to hide their bodies in long, conservative clothes anymore. They started wearing miniskirts—skirts that stopped well above the knee. Miniskirts were often paired with boots.

Step 1

Draw an arc for the shoulders. Add an oval for the head.

Step 2

Draw two vertical lines for the neck. Draw a rectangle for the body.

Step 3

Draw a curved line for the dress neckline. Add an arc for the miniskirt.

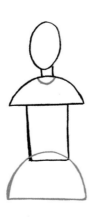

Step 4

Draw wavy lines for the hair. Draw four rectangles for the arms and two for the legs.

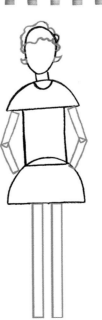

Step 5

Define the outfit with a sketch line. Add two arcs for the ears.

Step 6

Erase the extra lines. Add details such as a face, ovals for the belt, and tall boots.

Step 7

Color your person and add a background

Bell-Bottoms

In the late 1960s and early '70s, a lot of young men and women wore bell-bottom jeans. These jeans flared wide at the ankle to create a unique look.

Step 1

Draw a rectangle for the body. Add an oval for the head.

Step 2

Draw two vertical lines for the neck. Draw two rectangles for the legs. Add a crescent for the hair.

Step 3

Draw four rectangles for the arms. Draw two rectangles for the hands. Add two trapezoids for the bell-bottoms.

Step 4

Draw three triangles for the collar. Add two arcs and two rectangles for the shoes.

Step 5

Define the outfit with a sketch line. Define the hair with a wavy sketch line for the curly perm. Add two diagonal lines for the hands.

Step 6

Erase the extra lines. Add details such as a face, glasses, a mustache, and an oval for the belt buckle.

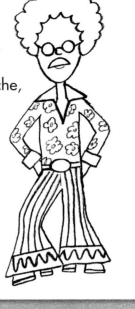

Step 7

Color your person and add a background.

Golf Shirts and Sweaters

The "preppy" look was popular in the 1980s. Men wore polo shirts, pleated khaki pants, and penny loafers with white socks. Women wore argyle socks and sweaters, corduroy shorts, and loafers. Both sexes often tied a sweater around their shoulders.

Step 1

Draw a rectangle for the body. Add an oval for the head.

Step 2

Draw two vertical lines for the neck. Draw two rectangles for the shorts. Draw a horizontal line for the waist.

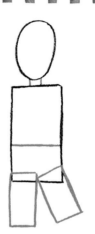

Step 3

Draw four rectangles for the arms. Add two triangles for the knee-high socks.

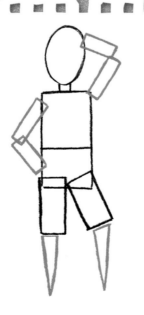

Step 4

Draw two triangles and a square for the sweater around the neck. Add straight lines to finish off the sweater.

Step 5

Define the outfit with a sketch line. Draw wavy lines for the hair. Draw an arc for one of the hands. Add two circles and a horizontal line for the glasses. Add two ovals for the shoes.

Step 6

Erase the extra lines. Add details such as a face, vertical lines for the pleats in the shorts, and a curved line for the hand in the pocket.

Step 7

Color your person and add a background.

Second-Hand Clothes

Second-hand clothing became popular in the 1990s. Untucked clothing in many layers, ripped pants, and a baggy, unkempt look was the style. "Grunge" dressers never wore designer labels. Fans of alternative rock music often sported the grunge style.

Step 1

Draw a rectangle for the body. Add an oval for the head.

Step 2

Draw four rectangles for the jeans. Add two ovals for the shoes.

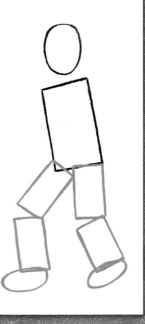

Step 3

Draw two vertical lines for the neck. Draw four rectangles for the arms.

Step 4

Draw an arc for the bandana. Add a square and a triangle for the shirt's neckline.

Step 5

Define the outfit with a sketch line. Draw two arcs for the hands. Add two triangles for the collar.

Step 6

Erase the extra lines. Add details such as a face, hair, and a guitar.

Step 7

Color your person and add a background.

The Band

To Learn More

At the Library

Abling, Bina. *Fashion Sketchbook*. New York: Fairchild Publications, 2000.

Maze, Stephanie. *I Want to Be a Fashion Designer*. San Diego: Harcourt Brace, 1999.

Tatham, Caroline. *Fashion Design Drawing Course: Principles, Practice, and Technique.*
 Hauppauge, N.Y.: Barron's, 2003.

On the Web

FactHound

FactHound offers a safe, fun way to find Web sites related to this book.

All of the sites on FactHound have been researched by our staff.

http://www.facthound.com

1. Visit the FactHound home page.
2. Enter a search word related to this book,
   or type in this special code: 1404811915.
3. Click on the FETCH IT button.

Your trusty FactHound will fetch the best sites for you!

Look for all the books in the Sketch It! series:
Drawing and Learning About ...

Bugs	Faces	Monsters
Cars	Fashion	Monster Trucks
Cats	Fish	
Dinosaurs	Horses	
Dogs	Jungle Animals